PILGRIM VOICES
Our First Year in the New World

Edited by Connie and Peter Roop
Illustrations by Shelley Pritchett

Walker and Company ✺ **New York**

First published in the United States of America in 1995 by Walker Publishing Company, Inc.

Published simultaneously in Canada by Thomas Allen & Son Canada, Limited, Markham, Ontario

Library of Congress Cataloging-in-Publication Data
Pilgrim voices ; our first year in the New World / edited by Connie and Peter Roop ;
illustrations by Shelley Pritchett.
p. cm.
Includes bibliographical references and index.
ISBN 0-8027-8314-7 (hc). — ISBN 0-8027-8315-5 (reinforced)
1. Pilgrims (New Plymouth Colony)—History—Juvenile literature. 2. Massachusetts—History—
New Plymouth, 1620—1691—Sources—Juvenile literature. [1. Pilgrims (New Plymouth Colony)
2. Massachusetts—History—New Plymouth, 1620–1691.] I. Roop, Connie. II. Roop, Peter.
III. Pritchett, Shelley, ill.
F68.P65 1995
974.4'8202—dc20   95-10114
CIP
AC

Book design by Chin-Yee Lai

Printed in Hong Kong

2 4 6 8 10 9 7 5 3 1

*For Mother and Father, in gratitude for all the joyous
Thanksgiving celebrations we have shared.*

Acknowledgments
The authors thank Carolyn Freeman Travers, director of research at
Plimoth Plantation, for sharing her invaluable expertise with us.

Foreword

The story of Plymouth Colony begins around 1606 in the small English village of Scrooby, Nottinghamshire, when a group of religious dissidents formed an independent church. They called themselves "Saints" and were called "Separatists" by others. At this time, the king of England was the head of the Church of England, and to separate from the Church meant treason. To avoid imprisonment or even death, in 1609 the Separatists fled to the Netherlands, where their religion was tolerated.

The Separatists lived first in Amsterdam and then moved to Leiden, where they were free to worship in their own way. As foreigners, however, their lives were difficult because jobs for them were scarce. Their poverty was such that no other Englishmen would join them. In 1618 a war between Spain and the Netherlands appeared possible, a war the Separatists did not want to be part of. At last, when their children began to act more Dutch than English, the congregation chose to emigrate once again, not to anyplace in Europe but to the new world of America.

After much discussion, the Separatists decided to colonize "the northern parts of Virginia" (which stretched north to what is now New York) around the mouth of the Hudson River. Negotiations resulted in a patent (grant of land) from the Virginia Company of London. Since the Separatists could not sponsor themselves, they formed a company. Merchants "adventured" (invested) money, and the colonists or "planters" adventured themselves. The Separatists planned to be a company for seven years. During this time, the merchants would supply them with necessary goods from England and the colonists would send back valuable goods to sell in England. The merchants also recruited other colonists ("Strangers") to join the Separatists.

Thus it was that on August 5, 1620, the *Speedwell* and the *Mayflower* set sail from Southampton, England, for America. However, the *Speedwell* proved unseaworthy and was abandoned, forcing the *Mayflower* to sail alone on September 6, 1620. The overloaded ship carried 102 passengers, of whom only 44 were Separatists.

After an arduous sixty-six day voyage, the *Mayflower* landed on the tip of Cape Cod. When it anchored, the area Native Americans, suspicious of Europeans, fired on an exploring party. No one was hurt in the exchange.

The local Indians had good reason to be wary of the Europeans. Previous to the *Mayflower*'s arrival, New England had been explored by Englishmen. Although several expeditions had been peaceable and profitable for both sides, one led by John Smith and Thomas Hunt was not. Hunt kidnapped twenty-seven men, including Squanto of the Nauset tribe, who lived near what is now Plymouth, Massachusetts. Fortunately for the future of the Plymouth Colony, the colonists were able to negotiate a peace treaty with Massasoit of the Pokanoket and other leaders. This peace remained unbroken for fifty-four years until King Philip's War in 1675.

Thus it was that a small group of Englishmen, venturing from England to Holland and then to America, searching for religious freedom, became the Pilgrims we know today.

Carolyn Freeman Travers
Director of Research
Plimoth Plantation

Editors' Note

Each year, at autumn's end, Americans celebrate Thanksgiving, a holiday closely linked to the Pilgrims. But who were these Pilgrims? Why were they escaping religious oppression in Europe? How did they fare crossing the Atlantic aboard a cramped and leaky *Mayflower*? What hardships did they face once they reached New England? How did the Pilgrims and Indians relate to one another? How many survived the struggles of the first year? How did the Pilgrims describe their first Thanksgiving celebration?

The Pilgrims answer these questions best in their own words from two histories: *Mourt's Relation* and *Bradford's History of Plymouth Plantation*. Most historians believe *Mourt's Relation* was written by the Pilgrims William Bradford and Edward Winslow.

Listen now as the Pilgrims, in their own words, tell the story of their first year in America.

6

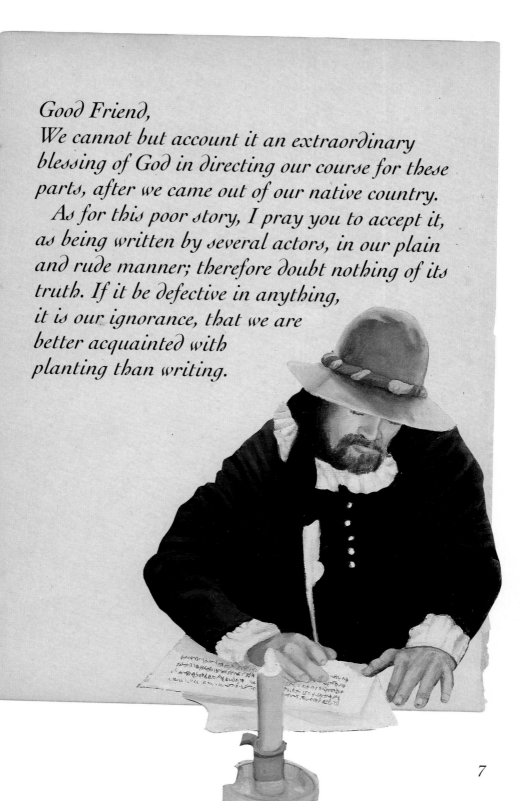

Good Friend,
We cannot but account it an extraordinary blessing of God in directing our course for these parts, after we came out of our native country.

As for this poor story, I pray you to accept it, as being written by several actors, in our plain and rude manner; therefore doubt nothing of its truth. If it be defective in anything, it is our ignorance, that we are better acquainted with planting than writing.

7

LEAVING

August 5, 1620: At length, after much travel and debates, all things were got ready and provided. A small ship (the *Speedwell*) was bought, and fitted in Holland, which was intended to serve to transport us and to use for fishing and such other affairs for the good and benefit of the colony.

We had not gone far, but Mr. Reinholds of the lesser ship complained that he found his ship so leaky as he could not put further to sea till she was mended. The ship was thoroughly searched from stem to stern, some leaks were found and mended, and now it was conceived by the

workman and all, she was sufficient, and they might proceed without either fear or danger. So with good hopes, we put to sea again, conceiving we should go comfortably on.

But it fell out otherwise, for after we were gone to sea again, the small ship was so leaky we could scarce free her with much pumping. So we resolved both ships to bear up back again and put into Plymouth. No special leak could be found, but it was judged to be the general weakness of the ship, and that she would not prove sufficient for the voyage.

September 6, 1620: Many troubles blown over, and now all being compact together in one ship (the *Mayflower*), we put to sea again with a prosperous wind, which continued many days together, which was some encouragement unto us; yet according to the usual manner many were afflicted with seasickness.

And, I may not omit here a special work of God's providence. There was a proud and very profane young man, one of the seamen, of a lusty, able body, which made him the more haughty. He would always be condemning the poor people in their sickness, and cursing them daily. But it pleased God before we came half seas over, to smite this young man with a grievous disease, of which he died in a desperate manner, and so was himself the first that was thrown overboard.

In all this voyage there died but one of the passengers, which was William Butten, a youth, servant to Samuel Fuller.

LAND

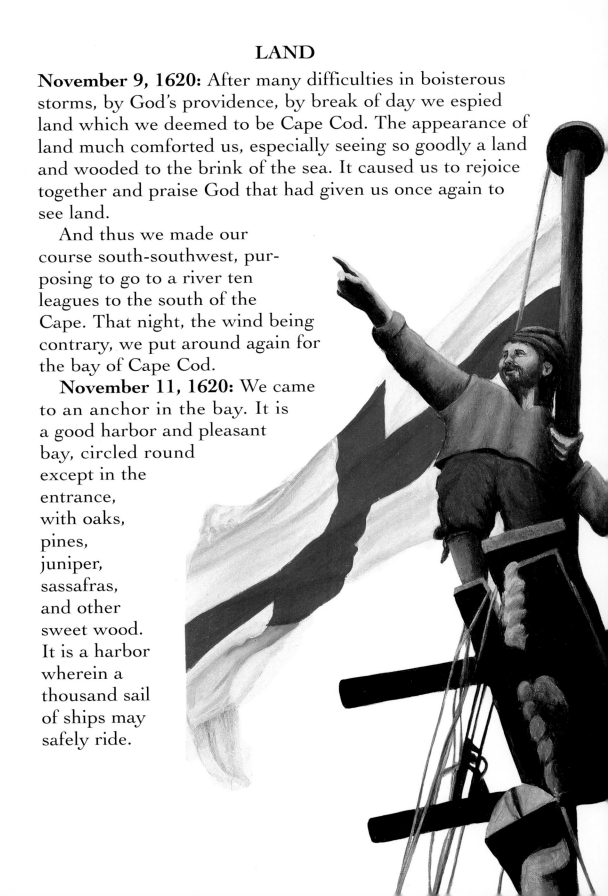

November 9, 1620: After many difficulties in boisterous storms, by God's providence, by break of day we espied land which we deemed to be Cape Cod. The appearance of land much comforted us, especially seeing so goodly a land and wooded to the brink of the sea. It caused us to rejoice together and praise God that had given us once again to see land.

And thus we made our course south-southwest, purposing to go to a river ten leagues to the south of the Cape. That night, the wind being contrary, we put around again for the bay of Cape Cod.

November 11, 1620: We came to an anchor in the bay. It is a good harbor and pleasant bay, circled round except in the entrance, with oaks, pines, juniper, sassafras, and other sweet wood. It is a harbor wherein a thousand sail of ships may safely ride.

MAYFLOWER COMPACT

Today, November 11, 1620, before we came to harbor, it was thought there should be an association and agreement. That we should combine together into one body, and submit to such government and governors as we should by common consent agree to make and choose.

IN THE NAME of God Amen. We whose names are underwriten, the loyall subjects of our dread soveraigne Lord King James by the grace of God, of great Britaine, Franc, & Ireland king, defender of the faith, &c.

Haveing undertaken, for the glorie of God, and advancements of the Christian faith and honour of our king & countrie, a voyage to plant the first colonie in the Northerne parts of Virginia, doe by these presents solemnly & mutualy in the presence of God, and one of another, covenant & combine our selves togeather into a civill body politick; for our better ordering, & preservation & furtherance of the ends aforesaid; and by vertue hearof to enacte, constitute, and frame shuch just & equall lawes, ordinances, Acts, constitutions, & offices, from time to time, as shall be thought most meete & convenient for the generall good of the Colonie: unto which we promise all due submission and obedience.

In witnes whereof we have hereunder subscribed our names at CapCodd the •11• of November, in the year the raigne of our soveraigne Lord King James of England, France, & Ireland the eighteenth and of Scotland the fiftie fourth. An°: Dom. 1620.

GOING ASHORE

Being brought safe to land, we fell upon our knees and blessed the God of heaven, who had brought us over the vast and furious ocean, and delivered us from all its perils and miseries.

Crossing the vast ocean, and the sea of troubles before in preparation, we now had no friends to welcome us, nor inns to entertain or refresh our weather-beaten bodies, no houses or much less towns to seek help.

What could now sustain us but the spirit of God and his grace?

We relieved ourselves with wood and water, and refreshed our people, while our shallop was fitted to coast the bay to search for a habitation. There was the greatest store of fowl that ever we saw.

We could not come near shore by three quarters of an English mile, because of shallow water, which was a great problem for us. Our people going onshore were forced to

wade to land, which caused many to get colds and coughs, for it was freezing cold weather.

The same day we set ashore fifteen or sixteen men, well armed, to fetch wood, for we had none left. We also wanted to see what the land was like, and what inhabitants we could meet with.

We found it to be a small neck of land. On the side where we lay is the bay, and far side the sea. The ground or earth has sand hills, much like the downs in Holland, but much better.

At night our people returned, but found not any person, nor habitation.

November 13, 1620: We unshipped our shallop and drew her on land, to mend and repair her. It was sixteen or seventeen days before the carpenter had finished her.

Our people went onshore to refresh themselves, and our women to wash, as they had great need.

EXPLORING THE LAND

November 15, 1620: We sent men ashore. We marched, single file, about a mile by the sea. We espied five or six people with a dog, coming towards us who when they saw us, ran into the wood and whistled the dog after them. First we supposed them to be Master Jones, the ship's master, and some of his men, but after we knew them to be Indians. Our men marched after them into the woods, lest other of the Indians would lie in ambush. But when the Indians saw our men following them, they ran away with might and main. We followed them that night about ten miles by the trace of their footings. At length night came upon us, so we set forth three sentinels. Some men kindled a fire, and others fetched wood.

In the morning so soon as we could see the track, we proceeded on our journey. We marched through boughs and bushes which tore our very armor in pieces. We could meet with none of them, not their houses, nor find any freshwater, which we greatly desired, and stood in need of, for we brought neither beer nor water with us. Our victuals was only biscuit and Holland cheese, and a little bottle of aqua vitae, so we were sore athirst. About ten o'clock we came into a deep valley and found springs of freshwater and sat us down and drunk our first New England water with as much delight as ever we drunk drink in all our lives.

When we refreshed ourselves, we directed our course to the shore and there made a fire that they in the ship might see where we were.

From thence we went on and found much plain ground, about fifty acres, fit for the plow, and some signs where Indians had formerly planted their corn. We found a little path to heaps of sand. One was covered with old mats and an earthen pot laid in a little hole at the end. We, musing what it might be, dug and found a bow and rotted arrows. We guessed there were many other things, but because we deemed them graves, we put the bow in again and made it up as it was and left the rest untouched, because we thought it would be odious unto them to ransack their sepulchres.

We went further on and found new stubble of this year's corn. We found where a house had been and a great kettle brought out of Europe. There was also a heap of sand made like the former, but it was newly done, for we could see how they had paddled it with their hands. We dug it up, and in it we found a little old basket full of fair Indian corn.

Digging further we found a fine new basket full of very fair corn of this year, with some thirty-six goodly ears of corn, some yellow, and some red, and others mixed with blue. After much consultation, we concluded to take the kettle and as much of the corn as we could carry away with us. When our shallop came, if we could find any of the people and speak with them, we would give them the kettle again, and satisfy them for their corn.

That night, we made a great fire and a barricade. We kept good watch with three sentinels all night, everyone standing when his turn came, while five or six inches of match was burning. It proved a very rainy night.

In the morning we lost our way. As we wandered, we came to a tree, where a young sapling was bowed down over a bow, and some acorns strewed underneath. Stephen Hopkins said it had been to catch some deer. As we were looking at it, William Bradford came upon it. As he went about it, it gave a sudden jerk up, and he was immediately caught by the leg. It was a very pretty device, made with a rope of the Indian's own making and having a noose as skillfully made as any roper in England.

In the end, we got out of the wood. We also did spring three partridges and we saw great flocks of wild geese and ducks.

At length, we came near the ship, shot off our pieces and the longboat came to fetch us. And thus we came both weary and welcome home, and delivered in our corn into the store, to be kept for seed, for we knew not how to come by any. This was our first discovery whilst our shallop was in repairing.

MORE EXPLORATION

November 17, 1620: When our shallop was fit, we set forth to make a more full discovery of the rivers. The wind was so strong the shallop was forced to harbor there that night. It blowed and snowed all that day and night, and froze withal. Some of our people that are dead took the origin of their death here.

The next day we sailed to the river formerly discovered which we named Cold Harbor. We found it not navigable for ships, yet thought it might be a good harbor for boats, for it flows there twelve foot at high water.

In the morning, we looked for the rest of the corn that we left behind when we were here before. This place we called Cornhill, and dug and found the rest, of which we were very glad. We went to another place and found more corn and a bag of beans, with a good many of fair corn ears. In all we had about ten bushels, which will serve us sufficiently for seed. And surely it was God's good providence that we found this corn, for else we know not what we should have done, for we knew not how we should find or meet with any Indians.

The next morning we followed certain beaten paths and tracks of the Indians supposing they would have led us into some town or houses. After five or six miles, we returned again another way, and found a grave much bigger and longer than any we had yet seen.

Whilst we were searching, two of the sailors espied two houses which had been lately dwelt in, but the people were gone.

The houses were made with long young saplings, bended and both ends stuck into the ground. They were made round, and covered down to the ground with thick and well-wrought mats. The door was not over a yard high, made of a mat to open. The chimney was a wide open hole in the top for which they had a mat to cover it close when they pleased. One might stand upright in them. Round the fire they lay on mats. There was also a company of deer's feet stuck up in the houses, hart's horn, and eagle's claws, also two or three baskets full of parched acorns, pieces of fish, and a piece of broiled herring. Some of the best things we took away with us, and left the houses standing still as they were. So, it growing towards night, and the tide almost spent, we hastened with our things down to the shallop, and got aboard that night, intending to have brought some beads and other things to have left in the houses, in sign of peace and that we meant to trade with them. But this was not done, by means of our hasty coming away from Cape Cod. But so soon as we can meet conveniently with them, we will give them full satisfaction. Thus is much of our second discovery.

THE THIRD DISCOVERY

A company was chosen to go out upon a third discovery. Whilst some were employed in this discovery, it pleased God that Mistress White was brought abed of a son, which was called Peregrine.

December 5, 1620: We, through God's mercy, escaped a great danger by the foolishness of a boy Francis, one of John Billington's sons. In his father's absence, he got gunpowder, made squibs, and shot them off in the cabin. With a loaded fowling piece, a little barrel of powder half full, and the fire within four feet of the bed and many people about the fire, and yet, by God's mercy, no harm was done.

December 6, 1620: We set out, being very cold and hard weather, for the water froze on our clothes and made them many times like the coats of iron.

In the morning, we divided our company, some eight in the shallop and the rest onshore to discover this place. We found great fish called grampus dead on the sand. They were cast up at high water, and could not get off for the frost and ice.

About five o'clock the next morning, we began stirring and two or three who doubted their pieces would go off shot them. After prayer, we prepared ourselves for breakfast and for a journey. Some said it was best not to carry the armor down to the shallop; others said they would be readier, two or three said they would not carry theirs till they went themselves. But the water was not high enough, so we laid the things down upon the shore and came up to breakfast. Anon, we heard a great and strange cry. One of our company cried, "They are men! Indians! Indians!" and withal, their arrows came flying amongst us. Our men ran out with all speed to recover their arms. In the meantime, Captain Miles Standish made a shot.

The cry of our enemies was dreadful, their note was after this manner, "Woach woach ha ha hach woach."

There was a lusty man and no whit less valiant, who was thought to be their captain, stood behind a tree within half a musket shot of us, and there let his arrows fly at us. He was seen to shoot three arrows, which all were avoided. He stood three shots of a musket. At length one took, after which he gave an extraordinary cry and away they all went.

Thus it pleased God to vanquish our enemies and give us deliverance. We called this place The First Encounter.

From thence we sailed all day along the coast. The seas had grew so great that we were much troubled and in great danger. Night grew on. Anon Master Coppin bade us be of good cheer; he saw the harbor. As we drew near, the gale split our mast in three pieces, and were like to have cast away our shallop. Yet, by God's mercy, we had the flood with us and struck into the harbor. We fell upon a place of sandy ground. We kept our watch all night in the rain upon this island.

On the Sabbath day we rested, and on Monday we sounded the harbor, and found it a very good harbor for our shipping. We marched also into the land, and found diverse cornfields, and little running brooks, a place very good for settling.

December 16, 1620: We put to sea again, and came safely into a safe harbor. This harbor is a bay greater than Cape Cod, compassed with goodly land, and two fine uninhabited islands. This bay is the most hopeful place, innumerable store of fowl, and excellent good fish in their season; skate, cod, turbot, and herring. We have tasted an abundance of mussels which are the greatest and best that ever we saw; crabs and lobsters, in their time infinite.

December 18, 1620: We went a-land. We marched along the coast in the woods, but saw not an Indian or Indian house; only we found where formerly had been some inhabitants, and where they had planted their corn. We found four or five small running brooks of very sweet, fresh water, that all run into the sea. Many kinds of herbs we found here in winter and an excellent strong kind of flax. Here is sand, gravel, and excellent clay for pots, and will wash like soap.

December 19, 1620: We went again to discover further.

After our landing and viewing of the places, we came to the conclusion, by most voices, to set on the mainland on the high ground, where there is a great deal of land cleared. There is a very sweet brook and many delicate springs of good water, and we may harbor our shallops and boats exceedingly well. Our greatest labor will be fetching wood, which is a half a quarter of an English mile. What people inhabit here we yet know not, for as yet we have seen none. So we resolved in the morning to come all ashore and to build houses.

December 21, 1620: It was stormy and wet. It was so tempestuous that the shallop could not go to land.

December 22, 1620: The storm still continued, that we could not get a-land nor those ashore come to us aboard ship. This morning Goodwife Allerton was delivered of a son, but it was dead born.

December 23, 1620: So many of us as could went onshore, felled, and carried timber, to provide themselves stuff for building.

December 28, 1620: We went to measure out the grounds for two rows of houses and a fair street. To greater families we allotted larger plots. So lots were cast where every man should lie, which was done and staked

out. We thought this proportion was large enough at first for houses and gardens considering the weakness of our people, many of them growing ill with cold.

Friday and Saturday, our people onshore were discouraged with the days being very stormy and cold.

January 9, 1620: We agreed that every man should build his own house. The common house, being near finished wanted only covering, it being about twenty feet square. Some should make mortar, and some gather thatch, so that in four days half of it was thatched. Frost and foul weather hindered us much, this time of the year seldom could we work half the week.

January 29, 1620: In the morning cold frost and sleet; both the longboat and the shallop brought our common goods onshore.

February 9, 1620: The cold weather continued, so that we could do little work. That afternoon our little house for our sick people was set on fire by a spark that kindled the roof, but no great harm was done.

MEETING THE INDIANS

February 16, 1620: It was a fair day, but the northerly wind continued the frost. One of our people was a-fowling about a mile and a half from our plantation and there came by him twelve Indians marching towards our plantation, and in the woods he heard the noise of many more. He lay close till they were passed, then with what speed he could, he went home and gave the alarm, so people in the woods returned and armed themselves, but saw none of them. Captain Miles Standish and Francis Cook, being at work in the woods, left their tools, but before they returned their tools were taken away by the savages. This coming of the savages gave us occasion to keep more strict watch, and to make our pieces ready.

February 17, 1620: Two savages presented themselves upon the top of a hill, about a quarter of a mile, and made signs unto us to come unto them. We likewise made signs unto them to come to us, whereupon we armed ourselves and stood ready, and sent two over the brook towards them. Only one of them had a musket, which they laid down on the ground in their sight as a sign of peace, and to parley with them, but the savages would not come.

February 21, 1620: The master came onshore with many of his sailors, and brought with him one of the great pieces called a minion and helped us to draw it up the hill with another piece that lay onshore. He brought with him a very fat goose to eat, and we had a fat crane, and a mallard, and a dried beef tongue and so we were kindly and friendly together.

March 16, 1620: Whilst we were busied hereabout, there presented himself a savage called Samoset, which caused alarm. He very boldly came all alone and along the houses straight to the rendezvous, where we intercepted him, not suffering him to go in, as undoubtedly he would, out of his boldness. He saluted us in English, and bade us welcome, for he had learned some broken English among the Englishmen that came to fish at Monhegan Island. We questioned him of many things. He said he was not of these parts, but of Morattiggon. The wind beginning to rise a little, we cast a horseman's coat about him, for he was stark naked only a leather about his waist, with a fringe. He had a bow and two arrows. Samoset was a tall, straight man, the hair of his head black, long behind, only short before, none on his face. He asked for some beer, but we gave him strong water and biscuit, and butter, and cheese, and pudding, and a piece of mallard, all which he liked well. He told us the place where we now live is called Patuxet, and that about four years ago all the inhabitants died of an extraordinary plague, and there is neither man, woman, nor child remaining. So there is none to hinder our possession or to lay a claim unto it.

All afternoon we spent in communication with him. We would gladly have been rid of him at night, but he was not willing to go this night. We lodged him that night at Stephen Hopkins's house, and watched him.

The next day he went away back to the Massasoits, who are our next bordering neighbors. The Nausets are as near southeast and those our people encountered. These people are ill affected towards the English, by reason of Hunt, a master of a ship, who took twenty out of this very place where we inhabit, and sold them for slaves.

MAKING PEACE

March 22, 1620: We met again about our public business, but we had scarce been together an hour, but Samoset came again with Squanto, the only native of Patuxet, where we now inhabit, who was one of the twenty captives that Hunt carried away and had been in England. They brought with them some few skins to trade, and some red herrings newly taken and dried. They signified unto us, that their great sagamore Massasoit was nearby, with Quadequina his brother, and all their men. We were not willing to send our governor to them, and they unwilling to come to us. So Squanto went again to them who brought word that we should send one to parley with him, which we did. Edward Winslow was to signify the mind and will of our governor, which was to have trading and peace with him. We sent to the king a pair of knives, and a copper chain with a jewel in it. To Quadequina we sent likewise a knife and a jewel to hang in his ear, and withal a pot of strong water, a good quantity of biscuit, and some butter, which were all willingly accepted. Our messenger made a speech unto him, that King James saluted him with words of love and peace, that our governor desired to see him, and to confirm peace with him, as his next neighbor. He liked well of the speech and heard it attentively, though the interpreters did not well express it.

After Massasoit had eaten and drunk himself, he came over the brook, and some twenty men following him, leaving all their bows and arrows behind them. We kept six or seven as hostages for our messenger. Captain Standish and Master Williamson met the king at the brook, with half a dozen musketeers. They saluted him and he them, and conducted him to a house being built where we placed a green rug and three or four cushions. Instantly

came our governor with drum and trumpet after him, and some few musketeers. After salutations, our governor kissing his hand, the king kissed him, and so they sat down. The governor called for some strong water, and drunk to him, and he drunk a great draught that made him sweat all the while after. He called for a little fresh meat, which the king did eat willingly, and did give his followers.

Then they agreed to peace which was:

1. *That neither he nor any of his should injure or do hurt to any of our people.*
2. *And if any of his did hurt any of ours, he should send the offender, that we might punish him.*
3. *That if any of our tools were taken away when our people were at work, he should cause them to be restored, and if ours did any harm to any of his, we would do the like to them.*
4. *If any did unjustly war against him, we would aid him; if any did war against us, he should aid us.*
5. *He should send his neighbors confederates, to certify them of this, that they might not wrong us, but might be likewise comprised in the conditions of peace.*
6. *That when their men came to us, they should leave their bows and arrows behind them, as we should do our pieces when we came to them.*

Lastly, that doing thus, King James would esteem of him as his friend and ally.

All of which the king seemed to like well. All the while he sat by the governor he trembled for fear. In his person, he is in his best years, an able body, grave in countenance, and spare of speech. In his attire little differing from his followers, only in a great chain of white bone beads about his neck.

March 23, 1620: Samoset and Squanto still remain with us. Squanto went to fish for eels; at night he came home with as many as he could well lift in one hand. They were fat and sweet and he caught them with his hands without any other instrument.

We chose our governor for this year, Master John Carver, a man well approved amongst us.

In these hard and difficult beginnings we found some discontents and murmurings arise amongst some, mutinous speeches; but they were soon quelled and overcome by the wisdom, patience, and just and equal carriage of things by the governor.

But that which was most sad was, that in two or three months' time half of the company died, especially in January and February, being the depth of winter, and wanting houses and other comforts; being infected with diseases, which this long voyage and their conditions brought upon us. Sometimes 2 or 3 died in a day; of 100 and odd persons, scarcely 50 remained. In time of most distress, we had but 6 or 7 sound persons, with abundance of toil and hazard to their own health, who did all necessary offices.

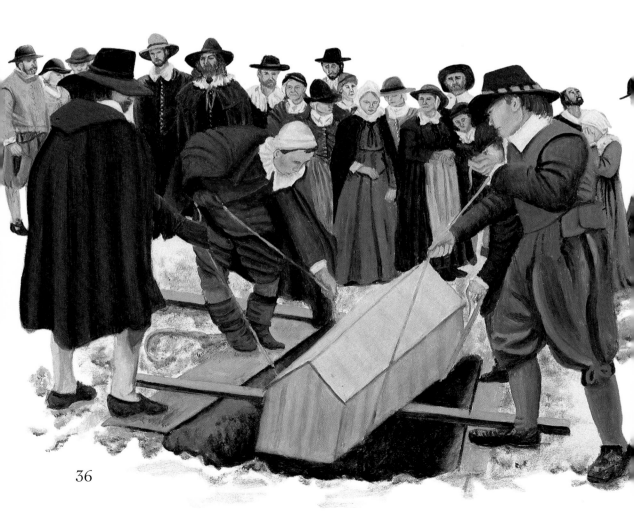

SPRING and SUMMER 1621

April, 1621: While busy planting, the governor, Mr. John Carver, came out of the field very sick. Within a few hours, his senses failed and he never spoke again. A few days after he died. His death was much lamented. He was buried in the best manner we could, with some volley of shot by all that bore arms. His wife died within five or six weeks after him.

Shortly after, William Bradford was chosen as governor, but he was not yet recovered of his illness, in which he had been near the point of death. Isaac Allerton was chosen to be his assistant.

May 12, 1621: Today was the first marriage in this place.

July 2, 1621: Mr. Edward Winslow and Mr. Hopkins, with Squanto as their guide, went to see our new friend Massasoit and bestow upon him some gifts to bind him faster unto us, view the country, and see in what manner he lived, and what strength he had about him. They found his place to be forty miles from hence, the soil good, and the people not many. Three years before, thousands of them died. They were not able to bury one another and their skulls and bones were found in many places laying still above the ground where their houses had been. A very sad spectacle to behold. A horseman's coat with some other small things were kindly accepted.

AUTUMN 1621

September 18, 1621: We sent out our shallop to the Massachusetts with ten men and Squanto for their guide and interpreter, to discover and view that bay, and trade with the natives. They returned in safety and brought home a good quantity of beaver.

We began now to gather in the small harvest we had and to fit up our houses and dwellings against the winter, being all well recovered in health and strength, and in all things in good plenty. Some fished cod, bass, and other fish, of which they took good store and of which every family had their

portion. As winter approached, we began to store food. Besides waterfowl, there was a great store of wild turkeys and venison. We had about a peck of meal a week to a person.

In this little time that few of us have been here, we have built seven dwelling houses, and four for the use of the plantation, and have made preparation for diverse others. We set the last spring some twenty acres of Indian corn, and sowed some six acres of barley and peas and according to the manner of the Indians, we manured our ground with herrings, or rather shads, which we have in great abundance.

THE HARVEST FESTIVAL

Our harvest being gotten in, our governor sent four men on fowling, that we might after a special manner rejoice together after we had gathered the fruit of our labors. They four in one day killed as much fowl as served the company almost a week. At which time, amongst other recreations, we exercised our arms. King Massasoit, with some ninety men, we entertained and feasted with for three days. They went out and killed five deer, which they brought to the plantation and bestowed on our governor, and upon the captain and others. And although it be not always so plentiful as it was at this time with us, yet by the goodness of God, we are so far from want.

We have found the Indians very faithful in their covenant of peace with us, very loving and ready to pleasure us. We often go to them, and they come to us; some of us have been fifty miles by land in the country with them. Yea, it hath pleased God so to possess the Indians with a fear of us, and love unto us. We walk as peaceably and safely in the woods as in the highways of England. We entertain them familiarly in our houses, and they as friendly bestowing their venison on us.

For fish and fowl we have great abundance, fresh cod in the summer. Our bay is full of lobsters all the summer. In September we can take a hogshead of eels in a night. Here are grapes, white and red, and very sweet and strong as well as strawberries, gooseberries, and raspberries.

NEW ARRIVALS

November 9, 1621: Thirty-five men put in at Cape Cod, some eight or ten leagues from us. The Indians that dwell there sent us word there was a ship near them.

They landed but with not so much as a biscuit cake or other food, neither had they any bedding. The plantation was glad of this addition of strength, but we wished that all of them had been better furnished with provisions.

We have sent goods by their ship *Fortune*, though it be not much, considering the smallness of our number all this summer. We hope the merchants will accept of it, and be encouraged to furnish us with things needful for further employment.

Advice for Future Pilgrims

As one small candle may light a thousand, so the light kindled here has shown unto many. We have noted these things so that you might see their worth and not negligently lose what your fathers have obtained with so much hardship.

Epilogue

Even though fifty mothers, fathers, sons, daughters, and friends died of pneumonia that first harsh winter in America, not one Pilgrim chose to return to England when the *Mayflower* set sail on April 5, 1621.

In November of that year thirty-five new settlers arrived on the ship *Fortune* without adequate clothing or food. The Pilgrims' first harvest no longer seemed as bountiful nor living space as plentiful with more hungry mouths to feed and people to house.

Hunger and limited supplies plagued the early settlers of Plymouth Colony. However, through courage and determination, the colonists survived. Key to their survival were the skills taught and the information provided by Samoset and Squanto. The colonists, mostly city dwellers, had little knowledge of farming or hunting. The Native Americans showed the Europeans how to plant native corn, how to catch eels and fish, and how to hunt game in their new country. The willingness of both the Native Americans and Europeans to live in friendship resulted in a peace that lasted fifty-four years.

At their harvest festival that year, the Pilgrims and Native Americans shared food and friendship. We now call this celebration "Thanksgiving." However, it wasn't until November 26, 1863, that President Abraham Lincoln proclaimed there be an annual "Thanksgiving Day" on the fourth Thursday in November.

Let us remember and celebrate the spirit of harmony, friendship, and gratitude that both the colonists and the Native Americans shared as they established our first Thanksgiving Day.

Glossary

a-fowling: hunting birds
anon: suddenly, soon, after a short time
arms: guns
aqua vitae: a type of strong liquor such as whiskey or brandy
bushel: 4 pecks or 32 quarts
draught: swallow
espied: noticed
extraordinary plague: bubonic plague
gale: large storm
grampus: a kind of whale
hogshead: unit of measure ranging from 62 to 140 gallons
league: 3 miles
minion: a type of cannon
Morattiggon: probably Monhegan Island in southeastern Maine
odious: offensive
parley: speak with
peck: 8 quarts
pieces: guns
Pilgrim: a "religious traveler." Bradford used this term once to describe the "Saints" ("Separatists" or "Brownists") who left England for the Netherlands
sagamore: leader
sepulchres: places of burial
shallop: an open boat with sails and oars
Stranger: name the "Separatists" gave to the colonists from London
strong water: any liquor
squib: explosive, early version of a firecracker
victuals: food

Bibliography

Primary Sources

Bradford, William. *Of Plymouth Plantation, 1620–1647*. Edited by Samuel Eliot Morison. New York: Alfred A. Knopf, 1952.

Mourt's Relation: A Journal of the Pilgrims at Plymouth. Edited with an introduction and notes by Dwight B. Heath from the original text of 1622. Cambridge/Boston: Applewood Books, 1986.

Secondary Sources

Arber, Edward. *The Story of the Pilgrim Fathers*. Edited from the original texts. 1897.

Fleming, Thomas J. *One Small Candle: The Pilgrims' First Year in America*, New York: Norton, 1964.

Usher, Roland Greene. *The Pilgrims and their History*. New York: Macmillan, 1918.

Willison, George F. *Saints and Strangers*. Time-Life Books, 1964.

The Pilgrim Reader. Garden City, N.Y.: Doubleday, 1953.

Source Information

Our primary sources were *Mourt's Relation* and Bradford's history *Of Plymouth Plantation*. Most historians believe William Bradford coauthored *Mourt's Relation* with Edward Winslow. *Mourt's Relation* is written in the first person. Bradford wrote his journal in the third person. In order to provide unity of voice, we changed Bradford's text to the first person. We modernized the language, including changes for clarity, in spelling, and in punctuation. We relied upon historians Dwight B. Heath and Samuel Eliot Morison for modern place names and dates. The dates in this book are original, so that the year changes on March 25 from 1620 to 1621 and the modern calendar grows further apart from the dates the Pilgrims recorded each year. Research for this book was conducted on site and in consultation with staff at Plimoth Plantation in Plymouth, Massachusetts.

Further Exploration for Young Readers

George, Jean Craighead. *The First Thanksgiving*. New York: Philomel, 1993.

Hayward, Linda. *The First Thanksgiving*. New York: Random House, 1990.

McGovern, Ann. . . . *If You Sailed on the Mayflower*. New York: Four Winds, 1969.

San Souci, Robert. *N. C. Wyeth's Pilgrims*. San Francisco: Chronicle, 1991.

Sewall, Marcia. *The Pilgrims of Plimoth*. New York: Atheneum, 1986.

Waters, Kate. *Samuel Eaton's Day*. New York: Scholastic, 1993.

——— . *Sarah Morton's Day*. New York: Scholastic, 1989.

Index